ONWARD✝

Biblical Beacons for the Christian Soldier's Journey

RC Atchisson

Printed in the United States of America

ISBN-10: 0-9864257-6-1
ISBN-13: 978-0-9864257-6-9

Stingy Brim LLC
St. Louis, MO 63123
www.rcatchisson.com

Cover Design by Jessica Sturgeon

All Scripture from the *King James Version of the Holy Bible, Old and New Testaments*

Onward, Christian soldiers!
Marching as to war,
With the cross of Jesus
Going on before.
Christ, the royal Master,
Leads against the foe;
Forward into battle,
See his banners go!

Traditional Hymn,
Sabine Baring Gould
(1865)

*L*et your light shine before men, that they may see your good works, and glorify your Father which is in Heaven.

--Matthew 5:16

Introduction

As an idea, "soldier" is a surprisingly fluid word, its meaning and attendant imagery varying from person to person.

For many it calls to mind a defender – of freedoms, of fairness, and of faith. The men and women who give of themselves to protect our beliefs, our lifestyles, and the things we hold nearest and dearest. Perhaps some picture John Wayne, or one of any number of other actors, ambling across the screen in a "Class C" field uniform dispensing wisdom and encouragement to his troops. For others it is much more personal. It is a father, mother, brother, sister, or friend enshrined in a picture on a mantle. Still others may harken back to grainy images of Civil War combatants, sporting either blue or grey depending upon the longitude and latitude of their homes or political sensibilities.

Most, though, rarely envision the friend, neighbor, or family member who quietly goes about their work of being a good citizen and a child of God. The unassuming nature and humble stewardship with which they daily attack the business of living as an example of the joy found in God's promise is often seen as anything but heroic. Yet, nothing could be further from the truth.

It is, no doubt, these very souls about whom lyricist Sabine Baring Gould wrote in 1865 when she penned the words to the classic hymn "Onward Christian Soldiers".

Based partially on II Timothy 2:3 ("Thou therefore endure hardness, as a good soldier of Jesus Christ."), the worship staple paints a vivid picture of the Church as God's army, thus making all people of faith "soldiers".

In this case, the soldiers are still fathers, mothers, brothers, sisters, and friends, but now they might be bakers, salesmen, postmen, preachers, teachers, or a host of other seemingly mundane occupations. Rather than find themselves dressed in olive drab or dress blues, these soldiers might wear smocks, suits, aprons, hard hats, or the collar of a clergyman. That symbolizes the true power of this army, for rather than find themselves armed with weapons and ammunition, these soldiers are armed with God's promise of salvation and His Word. What more could they need?

As it turns out...quite a lot. For as long as Christianity has existed, in whatever form, there has been opposition in the form of antagonists, agitators, and at least one persistent agent provocateur. Soldiers in the service of the Lord, then, are required to have fortified themselves with faith but the qualities of courage, wisdom, discernment, and righteousness just to name a few.

In a society growing increasingly more hostile toward the tenets that form the foundation of the Christian faith, and by extension then to the practitioners themselves, now more than ever it is important for those soldiers of faith to understand their role. That means understanding that passive worship has never been an option, for to truly worship requires service and that, by definition, is an active measure. It requires us to be good stewards, gracious neighbors, and obedient children of the Living God.

We are expected to serve one another as imitators of Christ's example. We are asked to forgive others as we have been forgiven. Our outward actions are meant to reflect humble and contrite hearts. Most importantly we are to do all of this in a spirit of love so that, as we are reminded in John 13:35, "By this shall all men know that ye are my disciples..."

So they will know that we are disciples. So they will know that we are soldiers...Christian soldiers...good soldiers of the Lord, Christ Jesus.

That is an idea on which all people of faith agree.

How to Use This Workbook

Unlike most devotionals, this is designed to be read and considered at your own pace as opposed to "X" page or pages per day. In theory, each Scriptural verse is meant to be read, considered, and prayed over for a month. The exercises (*Paraphrasing, What it Means, Food for Thought*) are supplemental and meant to spur reflection and exploration. Do one a day, one every other day, or do them all and once and go back over them if you so choose.

As stated before, a Bible and a dictionary are recommended. Additionally, there are volumes upon volumes of scholarly consideration and apologetic works that make for wonderful reading and instruction.

The most important thing to remember about the task at hand is to remember that this is a personal journey. Where you find yourself today may not be where you find yourself tomorrow. In a perfect world, you will have progressed, but disappointment and obstacles are a part of life. Sometimes they knock us back a step. Sometimes they knock us off of our feet entirely. Sometimes the winds of ill fortune will force us to change course. The key is to remember the end goal – Our Heavenly Father.

Should a setback occur, do not give up. Dig deeper -- both into Scripture and into yourself. Read and re-read. Most importantly, pray. Ultimately, the Truth that is the Word of God will resonate. The beacons He has shared with us will light your path.

In either case, it is up to you to make the journey...

The Soldier

The Journey *FOR* God

Fight the good fight of faith, lay hold on eternal life, whereunto thou art also called, and hast professed a good profession before many witnesses.

-     1 Timothy 6:12

H*ave not I commanded thee? Be strong and of a good courage; be not afraid, neither be thou dismayed: for the Lord thy God is with thee whithersoever thou goest.*

-- Joshua 1:9

Quick Note:
We have certain ideas and expectations about the qualities a good soldier must possess. Strength and courage surely top that list. Herein, though, we find that not only do those same qualities apply to the walk for God, they come FROM God as well.

Paraphrase

_____
_____
_____
_____
_____

Meaning

_____
_____
_____
_____
_____
_____
_____
_____
_____
_____

Food for Thought

The tone of this verse implies, to some measure, a lack of faith. Why do you think people sometimes find it difficult to trust in God's promises?

_____
_____
_____
_____
_____

What fears dominate your thoughts right now? In the short-term? Long-term?

_____
_____
_____
_____
_____

Why might it be so hard for many to move past the fear?

_____
_____
_____
_____
_____

Where and how has God "commanded" us previously on this topic?

_____
_____
_____
_____
_____

Do we have any reason not to believe Him? Explain.

_____
_____
_____
_____
_____

In what ways do we find God to be "with" us?

_____
_____
_____
_____

During which "fearful" moments of your life have you experienced His presence?

_____

_____

_____

_____

_____

How can this verse act as an important reminder about our role as Christian soldiers?

_____

_____

_____

_____

_____

How is our example important to those we meet?

_____

_____

_____

_____

_____

What is the "take away" most people would have of your day-to-day example?

_____

_____

_____

_____

_____

*T*hou preparest a table before me in the presence of mine enemies: thou anointest my head with oil; my cup runneth over. Surely goodness and mercy shall follow me all the days of my life: and I will dwell in the house of the LORD for ever.

-- Psalms 23:5-6

Quick Note:
It is in this verse that we are promised that the Lord will bolster us in the face of, or midst of, our enemies. The promise is not merely to survive but, indeed, to thrive. In fact, we are promised that, for as long as we live, we are graced by His kindness and His mercy. As soldiers in His cause, there is not more comforting assurance for which we could ask.

Paraphrase

_____
_____
_____
_____
_____

Meaning

_____
_____
_____
_____
_____
_____
_____
_____
_____

Food for Thought

Define "adversity" as you believe most people understand it.

_____

_____

_____

_____

_____

Suggest a definition of "adversity" as it applies to faith.

_____

_____

_____

_____

_____

Who is someone you consider to be an enemy? Why?

_____

_____

_____

_____

_____

What emotions do you find that your "enemies" elicit in you?

_____

_____

_____

_____

_____

What does it mean to be "anointed"?

_____

_____

_____

_____

_____

If we are so anointed, what responsibility do we have toward "enemies"?

_____

_____

_____

_____

_____

How might a table be "prepared for us"? Explain.

_____
_____
_____
_____
_____

Oh what two points does the Psalmist seem certain?

_____
_____
_____
_____
_____

What do you believe those points of certainty mean to the Psalmist?

_____
_____
_____
_____
_____

What do those certainties mean to you??

_____
_____
_____
_____
_____

*T*he wicked flee when no man pursueth: but the righteous are bold as a lion.

-- Proverbs 28:1

> **Quick Note:**
> *Herein, people are seemingly divided into two disparate camps: the Godly and the un-Godly. Their motivations appear to yield manifestly different reactions with the simile at the end speaking volumes about the confidence with which we should approach our calling.*

Paraphrase

_____
_____
_____
_____
_____

Meaning

_____
_____
_____
_____
_____
_____
_____
_____
_____
_____

Food for Thought

What does "righteous" mean to you?

_____
_____
_____
_____
_____

In what ways do you achieve or strive to achieve righteousness?

_____
_____
_____
_____
_____

How do you, personally, define "evil"? How does the dictionary define it?

_____
_____
_____
_____
_____

Describe the similarities and differences you notice in the definitions above.

_____
_____
_____
_____
_____

What is implied to cause, within the wicked, the urge to flee?

_____
_____
_____
_____
_____

Might "conscience" be the more popular term by which we call that impulse/introspection? Explain.

_____
_____
_____
_____
_____

What is the implicit of promise for the righteous?

_____
_____
_____
_____
_____

In what ways might the referenced boldness manifest itself?

_____
_____
_____
_____
_____

Why do you believe such boldness is warranted?

_____
_____
_____
_____
_____

Why might the writer of this verse have chosen the image of a lion?

_____
_____
_____
_____
_____

*B*ut they that wait upon the LORD shall renew their strength; they shall mount up with wings as eagles; they shall run, and not be weary; and they shall walk, and not faint.

-- Isaiah 40:31

Quick Note:
This verse reads like a pep talk from a coach...and what better coach to have than God, Himself? We are informed that we will soar like eagles, run without growing fatigued, and walk without exhausting ourselves. To make this promise manifest, all we need do is trust in the Lord.

Paraphrase

_____
_____
_____
_____
_____

Meaning

_____
_____
_____
_____
_____
_____
_____
_____
_____

Food for Thought

Here another promise is made to the faithful. How does it seem to differ than the others?

_____
_____
_____
_____
_____

The initial promise seems to yield three results – identify them.

_____
_____
_____
_____
_____

What is the importance of each?

_____
_____
_____
_____
_____

What possible symbolic importance can you identify for each?

_____
_____
_____
_____
_____

How does this promise align with the notion of free will?

_____
_____
_____
_____
_____

What is the importance of the word "wait" as it is used here?

_____
_____
_____
_____
_____

In what ways might we find our strength renewed?

_____
_____
_____
_____

Describe a time you felt you needed renewal.

_____
_____
_____
_____
_____

Describe how you felt when well-rested once again.

_____
_____
_____
_____
_____

How might you explain the importance of this verse to a non-believer?

_____
_____
_____
_____
_____

Behold, I send you forth as sheep in the midst of wolves: be ye therefore wise as serpents, and harmless as doves.

-- Matthew 10:16

> **Quick Note:**
>
> *Any good soldier depends upon a certain amount of strategy, generally direction given from the "higher ups" They don't come much higher up than God.*

Paraphrase

_____

_____

_____

_____

_____

Meaning

_____

_____

_____

_____

_____

_____

_____

_____

_____

Food for Thought

Identify the four animals that form the basis of the similes in this analogy.

_____
_____
_____
_____
_____

What characteristics do you associate with sheep?

_____
_____
_____
_____
_____

What characteristics do you associate with wolves?

_____
_____
_____
_____
_____

What characteristics do you associate with serpents?

_____
_____
_____
_____
_____

What characteristics do you associate with doves?

_____
_____
_____
_____
_____

Why might the impact of this analogy be lost on many people today?

_____
_____
_____
_____
_____

What in reality are we being cautioned about in the abstract?

_____

_____

_____

_____

_____

In what way(s) must we employ wisdom?

_____

_____

_____

_____

_____

In what way(s) must we employ peace?

_____

_____

_____

_____

_____

To what end must we utilize these two virtues?

_____

_____

_____

_____

_____

*B*ut love ye your enemies, and do good, and lend, hoping for nothing again; and your reward shall be great, and ye shall be the children of the Highest: for he is kind unto the unthankful and to the evil.

-- Luke 6:35

Quick Note:
This is a familiar refrain within the New Testament with many verses being a variation on the same or a similar theme. However, this particular passage seems particularly illustrative and emphatic in its point.

Paraphrase

_____
_____
_____
_____
_____

Meaning

_____
_____
_____
_____
_____
_____
_____
_____
_____
_____

Food for Thought

Describe some ways in which one might show love to his enemies.

_____
_____
_____
_____
_____

How might some misconstrue such actions (showing love to enemies) as a weakness?

_____
_____
_____
_____

In what ways is the reminder to expect nothing consistent with similar requests in Scripture?

_____
_____
_____
_____
_____

According to this verse, whom are we to emulate? Explain.

_____
_____
_____
_____
_____

Despite adhering to God's Word, what are some potential benefits of loving one's enemies?

_____
_____
_____
_____

What possible "reward" do we stand to gain? Explain.

_____
_____
_____
_____
_____

Soldiers are often taught to defeat an enemy. Does this verse challenge that notion? Explain.

_____
_____
_____
_____
_____

The word "enemy" implies conflict. What conflict might be at the heart of all others? Explain.

_____
_____
_____
_____
_____

Explain how it is possible a soldier might employ this philosophy, lose, and yet still win.

_____
_____
_____
_____
_____

Define "victory" as this verse intimates.

_____
_____
_____
_____
_____

*G**reater love hath no man than this, that a man lay down his life for his friends.*

--John 15:13

Quick Note:
A somber and stirring reminder of the cost of love. Soldiers of all stripes have learned this on some level or another.

Paraphrase

_____

_____

_____

_____

_____

Meaning

_____

_____

_____

_____

_____

_____

_____

_____

_____

_____

Food for Thought

Define "love" as you envision it.

_____
_____
_____
_____
_____

What is the dictionary definition of "love"?

_____
_____
_____
_____
_____

This verse seems to indicate that the ultimate sign of love is suffering a loss. What loss(es) have you suffered in the name of God? In His defense?

_____
_____
_____
_____
_____

To what degree of suffering would you willingly submit in defense of a friend? Your faith?

_____
_____
_____
_____
_____

Explain how you arrived at your answer to the question above?

_____
_____
_____
_____
_____

What does the word "friend" mean to you?

_____
_____
_____
_____
_____

Do you have different "levels" of friendship? Explain why or why not.

_____
_____
_____
_____
_____

How might your answer to the above affect how you view this verse?

_____
_____
_____
_____
_____

Though this verse is often interpreted in the traditional sense, it can very easily be viewed through the spectrum of the mundane. In what situations might that be the case in your life?

_____
_____
_____
_____
_____

A Christian soldier may simply be someone who acts as a defender of the faith in the role of an apologist, a steward, or simply a good and loving neighbor. What kind of cost might they suffer? Explain.

_____
_____
_____
_____
_____

*A*s it is written, For thy sake we are killed all the day long; we are accounted as sheep for the slaughter. Nay, in all these things we are more than conquerors through him that loved us

-- Romans 8:36-37

> **Quick Note:**
> *Though this verse seems to cast a pall over our charge, it is actually as inspirational as most verses you are like to find. It merely takes a bit more unpacking.*

Paraphrase

_____
_____
_____
_____
_____

Meaning

_____
_____
_____
_____
_____
_____
_____
_____
_____
_____

Food for Thought

Define "conquer":

_____
_____
_____
_____
_____

Once again, the sheep imagery is called upon. Why is that so often used? Why does it seem to be so apt a description?

_____
_____
_____
_____
_____

"All day long" could mean that numbers of people of faith are being killed, but it could also mean that we are repeatedly, metaphorically, "killed all day long". Explain how that can be so.

_____
_____
_____
_____
_____

"Slaughter" is a stark, loaded word. Why do you suppose such imagery is invoked in this verse?

_____
_____
_____
_____

What does "through him" mean in the context of this verse?

_____
_____
_____
_____
_____

What might someone be if they are "more than" a conqueror?

_____
_____
_____
_____
_____

The popular view of "conquer" means to vanquish or defeat a foe. However the Christian message is one of love. How might we do well to remember that with regard to conflicts in our daily lives?

_____

_____

_____

_____

_____

How is it possible to conquer though we might have appeared to lose?

_____

_____

_____

_____

_____

Christ's message of humility and service might seem to be at odds with the traditional image of a soldier, yet His word and message are eternal and true. How, then, would you explain this seeming dichotomy to someone who is not a person of faith?

_____

_____

_____

_____

_____

In what ways, according to Scripture, might you personally be better suited to serve as Christian soldier if you modified your approach to one of humility and love? In what situations?

_____

_____

_____

_____

_____

W *e are troubled on every side, yet not distressed; we are perplexed, but not in despair; Persecuted, but not forsaken; cast down, but not destroyed;.*

--2 Corinthians 4:8-9

Quick Note:
Though a glimpse at any newspaper might lead one to think otherwise, in Scripture we are told that our battles are not against flesh and blood, but instead against the powers, principalities, and rulers of darkness. Despite the pervasive nature of the foe and the power of the enemy to disrupt, we are reminded that in the end there is always hope in Christ Jesus' victory.

Paraphrase

_____
_____
_____
_____
_____

Meaning

_____
_____
_____
_____
_____
_____
_____
_____
_____
_____

Food for Thought

What troubles do you face in your life?

_____
_____
_____
_____
_____

How do you generally handle them when they arise?

_____
_____
_____
_____
_____

Is prayer a weapon in your arsenal? If not, why? If so, how so?

_____
_____
_____
_____
_____

What does it mean to be "troubled on all sides"? Explain.

_____
_____
_____
_____
_____

How would you define "perplexed"? Give an example.

_____
_____
_____
_____

How would you define "persecuted"? Give an example.

_____
_____
_____
_____

What does it mean to be "cast down"? Give an example.

_____
_____
_____
_____
_____

Despite these trials, what are we told, in this verse, that we are "not"?

_____
_____
_____
_____
_____

Explain the importance of what we are "not".

_____
_____
_____
_____
_____

How would you explain to non-believers in their own times of trial what we are "not"?

_____
_____
_____
_____
_____

*P*ut on the whole armour of God, that ye may be able to stand against the wiles of the devil. For we wrestle not against flesh and blood, but against principalities, against powers, against the rulers of the darkness of this world, against spiritual wickedness in high places. Wherefore take unto you the whole armour of God, that ye may be able to withstand in the evil day, and having done all, to stand. Stand therefore, having your loins girt about with truth, and having on the breastplate of righteousness; And your feet shod with the preparation of the gospel of peace; Above all, taking the shield of faith, wherewith ye shall be able to quench all the fiery darts of the wicked. And take the helmet of salvation, and the sword of the Spirit, which is the word of God: Praying always with all prayer and supplication in the Spirit, and watching thereunto with all perseverance and supplication for all saints; And for me, that utterance may be given unto me, that I may open my mouth boldly, to make known the mystery of the gospel,*

-- Ephesians 6:10-19

Quick Note:
Simply put: Our Marching orders.

Paraphrase

_____
_____
_____
_____

Meaning

_____
_____
_____
_____
_____

Food for Thought

List the pieces of the "armour of God" with which we are told to clad ourselves.

_____
_____
_____
_____
_____

Briefly describe the use / importance of each piece:

_____
_____
_____
_____
_____

What are the cornerstones we are called to utilize (not just the pieces, but what they represent)?

_____
_____
_____
_____
_____

There is an urgency in this call to arms. Is that urgency as apparent today? Need it be? Explain.

_____
_____
_____
_____
_____

Despite the description of a combatant going to war, this passage reads like a defensive guide. Explain why you agree or disagree with that statement.

_____
_____
_____
_____
_____

Against whom or what are we seemingly defending ourselves?

_____
_____
_____
_____
_____

With which of these pieces do you feel well-equipped during this season of your life? Why?

_____

_____

_____

_____

_____

How can you better equip yourself for those elements you find lacking?

_____

_____

_____

_____

_____

What is the essence of this call to arms? In other words, what are we being encouraged to do?

_____

_____

_____

_____

_____

How might we best do that?

_____

_____

_____

_____

_____

I *can do all things through Christ which strengtheneth me.*

-- Phillipians 4:13

Quick Note:
Perhaps this is best understood on the heels of the previous verse. If nothing else, it is certainly an encouraging addendum to not only the preceding verse but all other verses encouraging us to be patient, steadfast, and strong.

Paraphrase

_____
_____
_____
_____
_____

Meaning

_____
_____
_____
_____
_____
_____
_____
_____
_____

Food for Thought

On a basic level do you truly believe the sentiment of the verse? Why or why not?

_____
_____
_____
_____
_____

What limitations, if any, might the truth of this verse present to some?

_____
_____
_____
_____
_____

Are those limitations an argument against the power of God? Explain.

_____
_____
_____
_____
_____

In what way(s) does Christ "strengthen" us?

_____
_____
_____
_____
_____

How might this phrase be misinterpreted by some?

_____
_____
_____
_____

What is something you have always dreamed or hoped you would accomplish yet did/have not?

_____
_____
_____
_____

Upon reflection, why did/have you not accomplished it?

_____
_____
_____
_____
_____

How does this verse relate, then, to that failure?

_____
_____
_____
_____
_____

How might this phrase be more prescriptive of what we may endure rather than accomplish?

_____
_____
_____
_____
_____

How might you explain the importance of this verse to someone who is not a person of faith?

_____
_____
_____
_____
_____

***B**ut sanctify the Lord God in your hearts: and be ready always to give an answer to every man that asketh you a reason of the hope that is in you with meekness and fear:*

-- 1 Peter 3:15

Quick Note:
Quite simply...our mission.

Paraphrase

_____
_____
_____
_____
_____

Meaning

_____
_____
_____
_____
_____
_____
_____
_____
_____

Food for Thought

What does "sanctify" mean to you?

_____

_____

_____

_____

_____

What is the dictionary definition of "sanctify"?

_____

_____

_____

_____

_____

How may we, as people of faith, accomplish the opening charge of this verse? Give examples.

_____

_____

_____

_____

_____

What is the "hope" to which this verse refers?

_____

_____

_____

_____

_____

Many are afraid to defend their faith when called upon to do so. Why might that be?

_____

_____

_____

_____

_____

In what way(s) must we effectively prepare ourselves to give an answer when asked?

_____

_____

_____

_____

_____

God's promise of salvation through Christ is for all, yet many do not wish to hear it much less believe it. How might we best approach that two-fold challenge?

_____
_____
_____
_____
_____

In this verse we are called to give answer in the spirit of humility. Why do so many seem to have a problem answering this call in that spirit?

_____
_____
_____
_____
_____

Why might it be important that this verse states that we give reason for our faith once we have been asked? Does that mean we should not offer unsolicited opinions on the gift of Christ? Explain.

_____
_____
_____
_____
_____

How might you argue that this is the single most important role of a Christian soldier?

_____
_____
_____
_____
_____

*T*he grace of our Lord Jesus Christ be with you all. Amen.

-- Revelation 22:21

Living Water

Did you know that almost 800 million people worldwide lack access to clean drinking water?

To date, Living Water International has completed over 15,000 water projects in 26 countries. Just by purchasing this book you have already helped them in their efforts as 10% of all profits are being donated, but I hope you would consider additional support – either individually or with the help of an organization or community to which you belong.

For more information about the great folks at Living Water International and their mission, please visit www.water.cc .

About the Author

RC Atchisson is a Midwest native, born and raised in St. Louis, Missouri. A teacher for almost 20 years, he has written for print, radio, television, and film. In addition, he has produced a variety of independent and live theatrical projects. Visit www.rcatchisson.com to learn more about upcoming projects and productions.